PIANO
VOCAL
GUITAR

THROUGH THE YEARS
The Songs of
STEVE DORFF

Thanks to all of my wonderful co-writers
who I've had the privilege of working with
over the years, and to all of the amazing artists
that have honored me by recording my work.

This book is dedicated to
Stephen, Andrew, Callie and Kaitlyn.

Official website: **www.stevedorff.com**

Cover photos by Pixel Planet

ISBN 978-1-4234-9378-5

7777 W. BLUEMOUND RD. P.O. BOX 13819 MILWAUKEE, WI 53213

Visit Hal Leonard Online at
www.halleonard.com

BIOGRAPHY

Industry observers have dubbed multiple award-winning Steve Dorff an enigma who has evolved into a gifted composer in every musical field. There is no way to capture the diversity he regularly displays scoring major motion pictures, television, theater, or via an array of #1 hit songs. In addition to winning the NSAI Songwriter of the Year award, Dorff has also been honored with more than 40 BMI and 11 *Billboard* #1 awards.

Born and raised in New York City, Dorff began composing music before he ever learned how to play the piano. From a very young age, he was constantly inspired by the everyday, leading him to underscore the vibrant goings-on all around him.

His was a formidable breakthrough, accelerated through a highly productive association with the legendary Clint Eastwood, beginning with "Every Which Way but Loose." This out-of-the-box smash soon paved the way for a raft of compositions reflecting all musical genres, from contemporary sounds to haunting orchestral melodies.

Three-time GRAMMY® nominee and a fixture on the nation's charts, his dossier includes nine #1 film songs and 15 Top 10 hits, including the Kenny Rogers classic "Through the Years," a BMI 3-million-performance song, as well as "I Just Fall in Love Again," the Anne Murray record that captured *Billboard's* #1 Song Of The Year honor. His many songs have been sung by some of the greatest artists of our time—Barbra Streisand, Celine Dion, Whitney Houston, George Strait, Vanessa Williams and countless others.

Emmy® nominee for five television compositions, his credits are exemplary and include such standards as "Murphy Brown" and "Murder, She Wrote." You'll also find his name on evergreens like "Growing Pains," "Alien Nation," "Spenser: For Hire," "Major Dad", "Columbo," "Reba" and the CMT hit "The Singing Bee."

His many TV and cable movie credits include the Emmy-nominated CBS mini-series *Elvis*, the Hallmark Hall of Fame *Rose Hill*, the animated Christmas classic *Annabelle's Wish*, *Babe Ruth*, *The Quick and the Dead*, *Moonshine Highway* and *The Defiant Ones*. Dorff's many movie songs and scores have been featured in *Bronco Billy*; *Blast From The Past*; *Rocky IV*; *Pure Country*; *Tin Cup*; *Michael*; *Dudley Do-Right*; *Dancer, Texas*; *The Last Boy Scout*; *Curly Sue*; and *Honky Tonk Man*.

Perhaps Dorff's most ambitious move to date has been a giant leap into his first love, musical theater. He has two projects making their way to the stage: *Josephine (The Josephine Baker Story)* and *Pure Country (The Musical)*.

CONTENTS

ANOTHER HONKY TONK NIGHT ON BROADWAY

Words and Music by STEVE DORFF,
MILTON BROWN and SNUFF GARRETT

Medium Country Western

HYPNOTIZE THE MOON

Words and Music by STEVE DORFF
and ERIC KAZ

hyp - no - tize ____ moon. ____

D.S. al Coda

You

CODA

charm the stars, ____ she could charm the stars, ____

hyp - no - tize ____ the moon. ____

rit.

ANY WHICH WAY YOU CAN

Words and Music by STEVE DORFF
and MILTON BROWN

Moderately slow Ballad

once a - gain.__ You'll leave with a prom-ise you'll call me to - mor - row, but

I nev - er know__ when the next time will be.__ And each time you leave me I

can't help but won - der, was to-night__ the last night__ for you__ and for me?__

Chorus:

An - y which way you__ can, just love me an - y which way you__

AS LONG AS WE GOT EACH OTHER

from GROWING PAINS

Words and Music by JOHN BETTIS
and STEVE DORFF

Show me that smile— a - gain,— don't waste an - oth - er min -
When - ev - er skies— are grey — I look in - to— your eyes—
Instrumental

ute on your cry - in'. We're no - where near— the end,— the best—
— and see them shin - in'. Hold - ing you close— this way— is like—

COCA COLA COWBOY

Words and Music by STEVE DORFF,
JAMES PINKARD JR., IRVING DAIN
and SAMUEL ATCHLEY

COWBOYS AND CLOWNS

Words and Music by STEVE DORFF,
GARY HARJU, LARRY HERBSTRITT
and SNUFF GARRETT

Moderately slow, with expression

clowns.

Cow-boys love can-dle-light___ and lac-y things___ on la-dies while

kids love ca-rous-els___ and fun-ny paint-ed fac-es. But there's

no bal-loons, no sweet per-fume___ when mid-night brings you down,___ no one to

DON'T UNDERESTIMATE MY LOVE FOR YOU

Words and Music by DAVE LOGGINS,
STEVE DIAMOND and STEVE DORFF

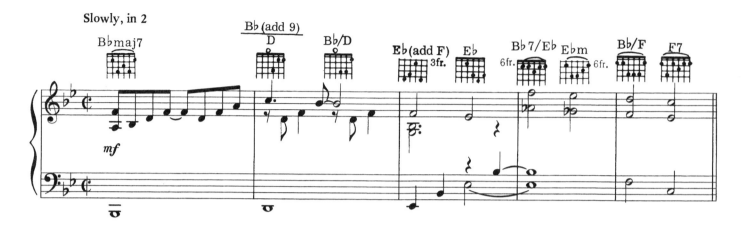

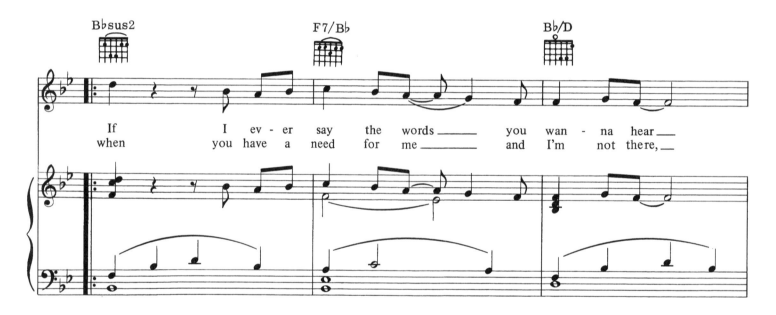

If I ev - er say the words _____ you wan - na hear _____
when you have a need for me _____ and I'm not there, _____

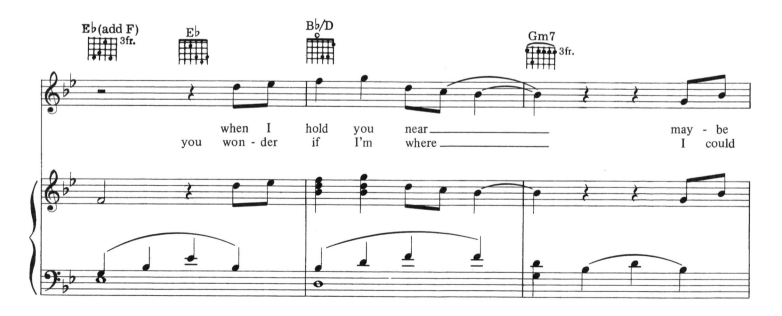

when I hold you near _____ may - be
you won - der if I'm where _____ I could

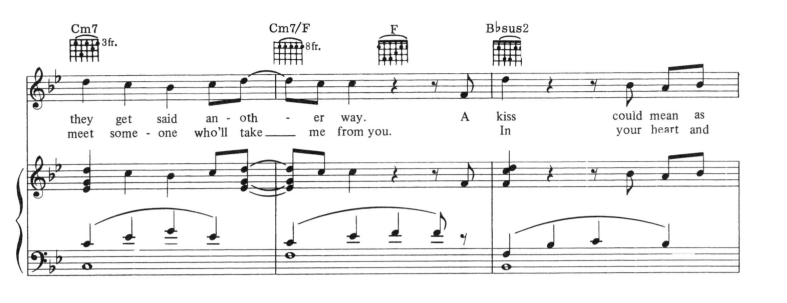

they get said an - oth - er way. A kiss could mean as
meet some - one who'll take___ me from you. In

much for me___ as words could ev - er do.___ You know I
soul you know___ I'm the one thing you can't lose.___

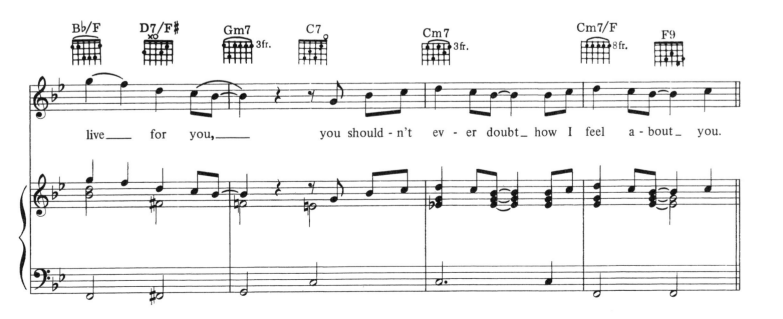

live___ for you,___ you should - n't ev - er doubt_ how I feel a - bout_ you.

EVERY WHICH WAY BUT LOOSE

from EVERY WHICH WAY BUT LOOSE

Words and Music by STEVE DORFF,
MILTON BROWN and THOMAS GARRETT

Moderate Country

I've al-ways been the kind _ of man _ who does-n't be-lieve _ in strings. _

Long-term _ ob-li-ga-tions are just un-nec-es-sar-y things. _ But,

girl, you've got me think-in', while I'm drink-in' _ one more _ beer. _ If I'm

feel the need to hold you close and love the night a - way, ___ while you're
hur - ry if they want me, 'cause I can feel me fad - ing fast, ___ while you're

turn - ing ___ me ___ ev - 'ry which way ___ but loose. ___ You turn me

ev - 'ry which way ___ but loose. ___ In - side the fi - re's burn - ing ___ me. In my ___

mind you just keep _ turn - ing me _ ev - 'ry which way _ but loose. _

Ba - by, there's no _ ex - cuse. _ You turn me ev - 'ry _ which way _ but

loose. _ When the loose. _

HEARTLAND

Words and Music by STEVE DORFF
and JOHN BETTIS

Moderate Country

When you hear twin fid - dles and a steel gui - tar, ___

you're lis - t'nin' to the sound of the A -

mer - i - can heart. And Op - ry mu - sic on a

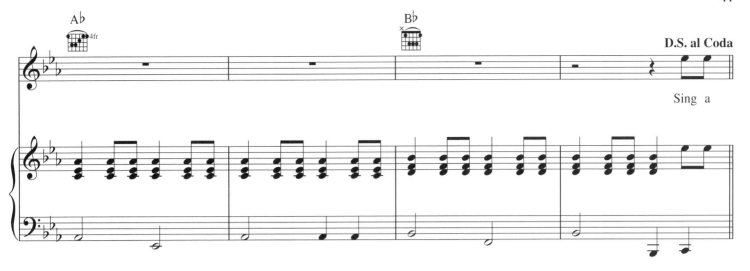

D.S. al Coda

Sing a

CODA

life.

N.C.

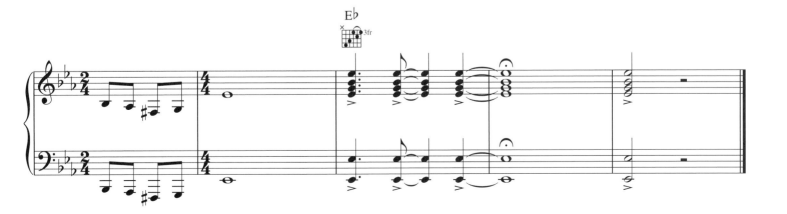

HIGHER GROUND

Words and Music by STEVE DORFF,
GEORGE GREEN and CHARLES AGEE

Walk me o - ver this __ ho - ri - zon. __
I have walked __ too long __ in dark - ness. __

Let the sun's __ light warm my face. __
I have walked __ too long a - lone, __

I CROSS MY HEART

from the Warner Bros. film PURE COUNTRY

Words and Music by STEVE DORFF
and ERIC KAZ

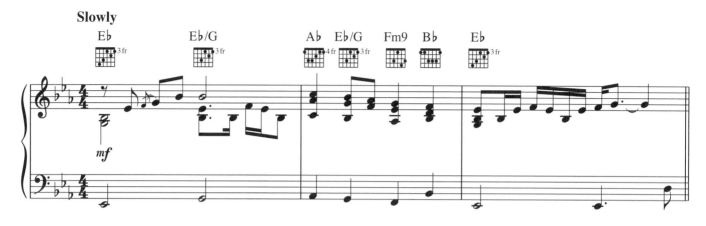

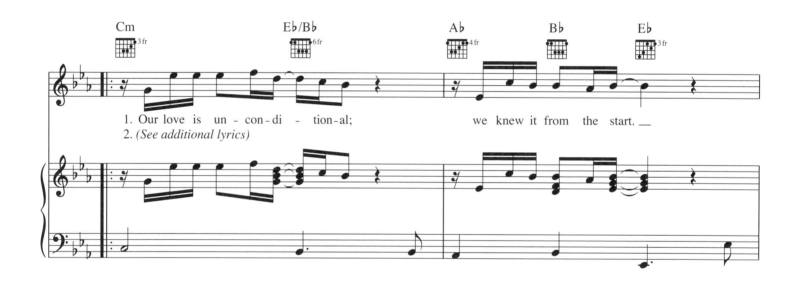

1. Our love is un-con-di - tion-al; we knew it from the start.
2. (See additional lyrics)

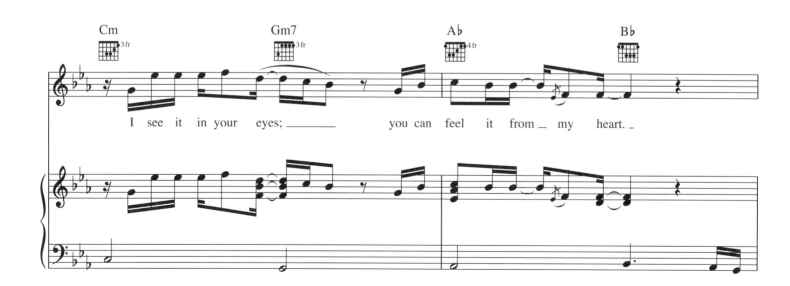

I see it in your eyes; _____ you can feel it from _ my heart. _

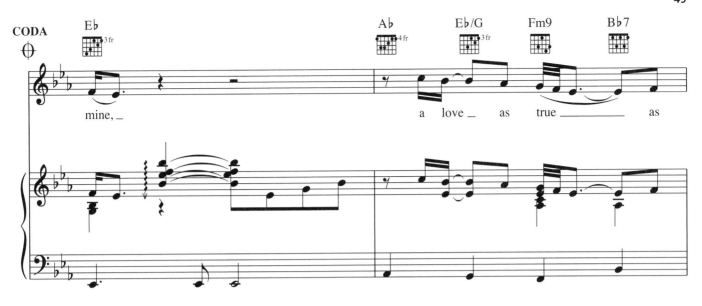

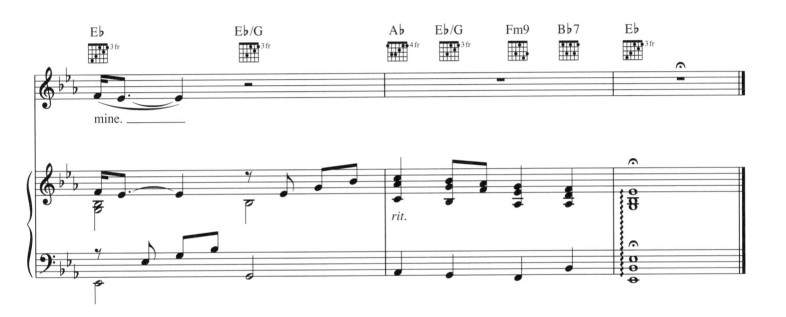

Additional Lyrics

2. You will always be the miracle
   That makes my life complete;
   And as long as there's a breath in me,
   I'll make yours just as sweet.
   As we look into the future,
   It's as far as we can see,
   So let's make each tomorrow
   Be the best that it can be.
   Chorus

I DON'T THINK I'M READY FOR YOU

Words and Music by STEVE DORFF, MILTON BROWN,
BURT REYNOLDS and SNUFF GARRETT

I JUST FALL IN LOVE AGAIN

Words and Music by LARRY HERBSTRITT,
STEVE DORFF, GLORIA SKLEROV
and HARRY LLOYD

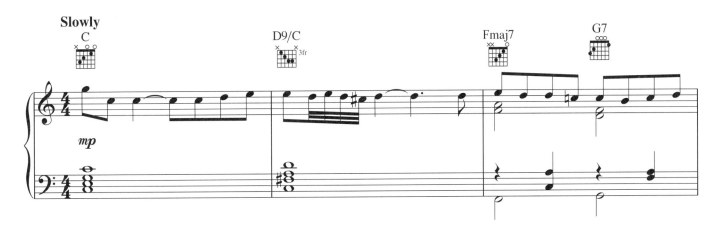

Dream-in', I must be dream-in'; or
Mag-ic, it must be mag-ic; the way I

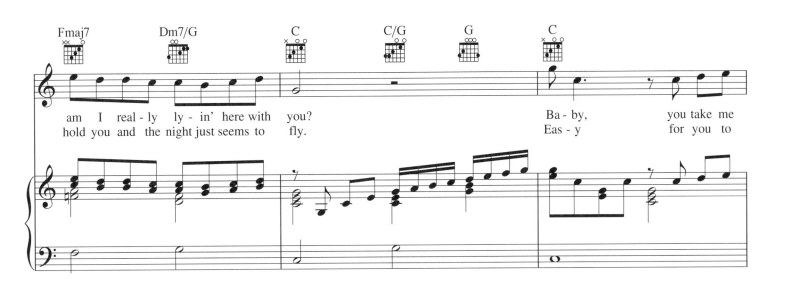

am I real-ly ly-in' here with you? Ba-by, you take me
hold you and the night just seems to fly. Eas-y for you to

I'LL WAKE YOU UP WHEN I GET HOME

Words and Music by STEVE DORFF
and MILTON BROWN

LASSO THE MOON
from the Movie RUSTLER'S RHAPSODY

Words and Music by STEVE DORFF
and MILTON BROWN

THE MAN IN LOVE WITH YOU

Words and Music by STEPHEN DORFF
and GARY HARJU

I'm not the he - ro ___ who will
I'm not the key ___ that
So when the world won't turn the

al - ways save the day.
o - pens ev - 'ry door.
way you wish it would

Don't al - ways wear the white hat, ___ don't
I don't have the pow - er ___ to give you
and the dreams you have don't come a - live as

MIRACLE

Words and Music by STEVE DORFF
and LINDA THOMPSON

1. You're my life's___ one mir - - a - cle,
2. You're the reas - on I___ was born.
3. When you smile___ at me,___ I cry.

ev - 'ry - thing I've done_____ that's good, and you
Now I fi - n'ly know___ for sure. And I'm
And to save your life,_____ I'd die. With a

* Original recording in key of F♯ Major.

MY HEART WILL NEVER KNOW

Words and Music by STEVE DORFF
and BILLY KIRSCH

Moderate ballad

I poured two cups of cof - fee, put the

It's been a long, cold De - cem - ber, the

pa - per on the ta - ble so we can share the morn - ing

snow out - side keeps fall - ing. I'll light a fire when you get

ROSE HILL SUITE

By STEVE DORFF

Moderately

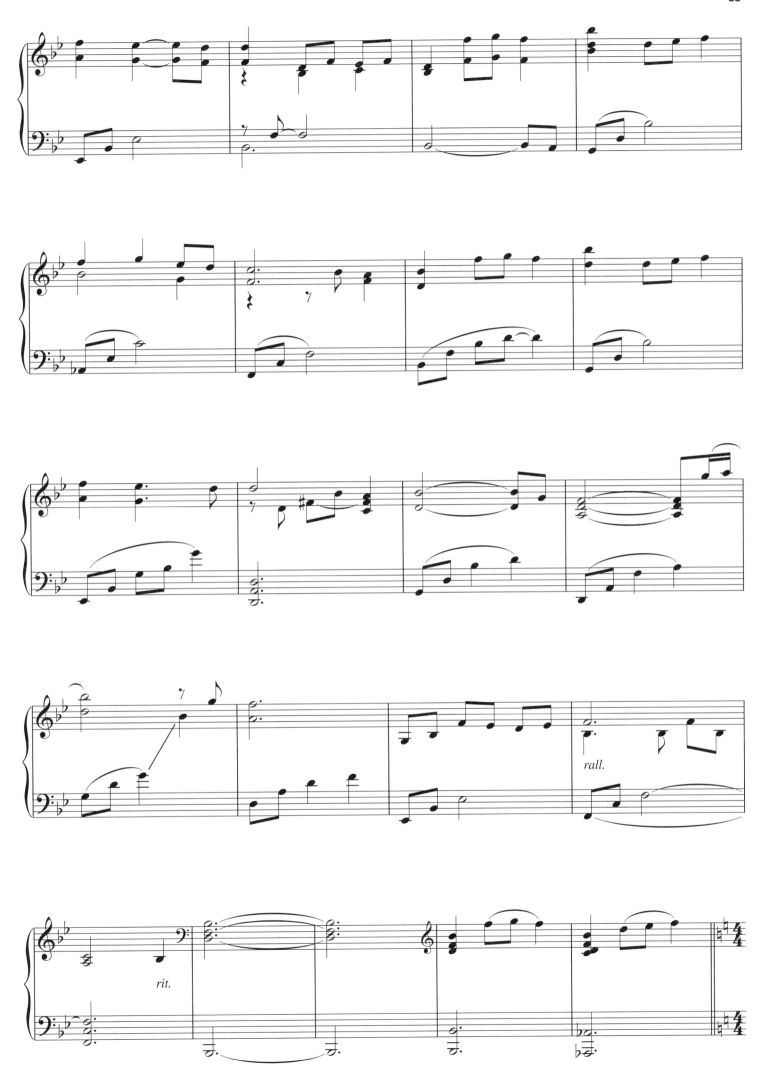

SHE USED TO BE MINE

Words and Music by STEVE DORFF
and MARTIN PANZER

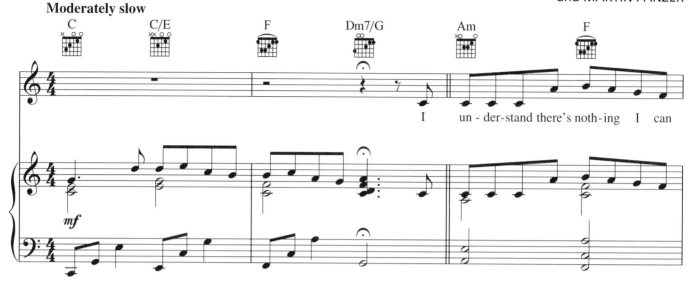

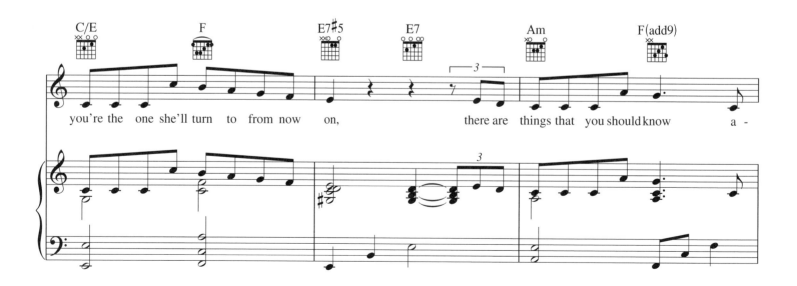

SPENSER FOR HIRE

Words and Music by STEVE DORFF
and LARRY HERBSTRITT

Medium Rock

SWEPT AWAY

Words and Music by CHRISTOPHER CROSS,
STEVE DORFF and JOHN BETTIS

TAKE GOOD CARE OF MY HEART

Words and Music by STEVE DORFF
and PETER McCANN

Time can pass ___ so slow-
Come and make ___ your mag-

-ly when you feel so all ___ a-lone.
-ic till you have me hyp-no-tized.

THROUGH THE YEARS

Words and Music by STEVE DORFF
and MARTY PANZER

THE WORLD FROM WAY UP HERE
(Annabelle's Wish)

Words and Music by STEVE DORFF
and JOHN BETTIS

Wish I may, ___ wish I might, ___
Moun-tain high, ___ val-ley low, ___

on my fa - v'rite star. ___
where the wind ___ is free. ___

Let me feel, ___
I will feel, ___

let me see ___ the world from where ___ you are. ___
I will know ___ the world the an - gels see. ___

PACIFIC SUNRISE

By STEVE DORFF

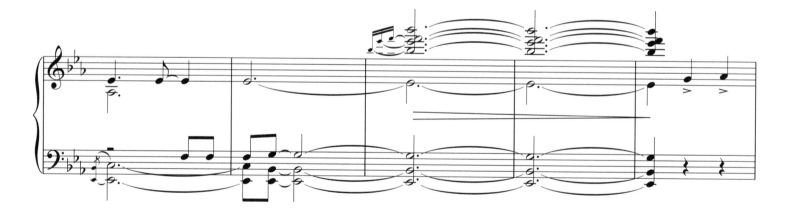

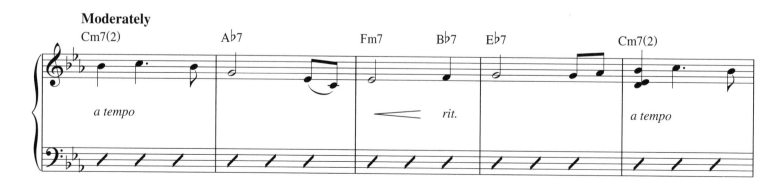

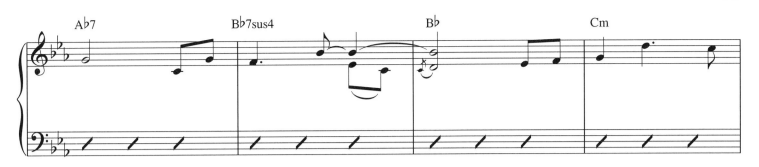

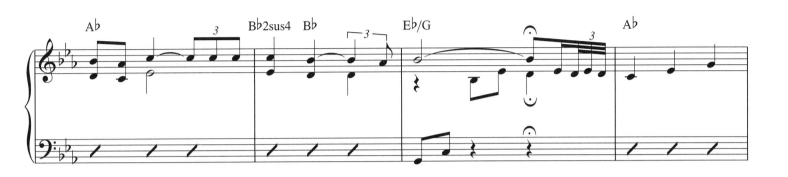